The Resurrection and You

The Resurrection and You

How the Resurrection Answers
Your Biggest Questions

DEVEN K. MACDONALD

RESOURCE *Publications* · Eugene, Oregon

THE RESURRECTION AND YOU
How the Resurrection Answers Your Biggest Questions

Copyright © 2022 Devin K. MacDonald. All rights reserved. Except for brief quotations in critical publications or reviews, no part of this book may be reproduced in any manner without prior written permission from the publisher. Write: Permissions, Wipf and Stock Publishers, 199 W. 8th Ave., Suite 3, Eugene, OR 97401.

Resource Publications
An Imprint of Wipf and Stock Publishers
199 W. 8th Ave., Suite 3
Eugene, OR 97401

www.wipfandstock.com

PAPERBACK ISBN: 978-1-6667-3643-4
HARDCOVER ISBN: 978-1-6667-9469-4
EBOOK ISBN: 978-1-6667-9470-0

MAY 27, 2022 11:50 AM

To my wife, Heather. Thank you for modeling the truth and the transforming power of the resurrection in everyday life. You make marriage easy. All my love, forever.

Contents

Acknowledgments | ix

Abbreviations | xi

1 Introduction | 1
2 The Non-Negotiables | 8
3 Alternative Explanations for the Resurrection | 19
4 Evidence for the Resurrection | 30
5 How the Resurrection Answers Our Big Questions | 39
6 The Resurrection of Jesus Is Not Just True, It's Transformational | 48
7 The Resurrection and You | 57

Bibliography | 61

Scripture Index | 63

Acknowledgments

I'D like to make it a point to thank several people and to ask forgiveness of anyone I've omitted or overlooked in doing so! There are too many people to recognize, even for a short work such as this.

Thank you to those who provided an initial review and careful read of the first draft: Rev. Nathan Klahsen, Pastor Luke Cuthbert, Nathan Scott, and Tyler Legouffe for help with design. Thank you as well to Matthew Damstra for his early help in compiling some research and in the preliminary transcription process. My editor, Kerry Wilson, did a fantastic job of ensuring consistency across the board. It was a pleasure to work with Kerry, and I look forward to future projects together. Any mistakes in print are entirely my fault.

To the elders and staff at Summerside Community Church, I am deeply grateful, not only to serve alongside you, but also for the room, space, and quiet that you provided for me in the writing process. I am forever indebted to Rev. Mark Cuthbert for his wisdom, input, and advice on this and every other project (not to mention for allowing me access to his theological library). Thank you also to Liz Fildey for daily help in countless ways. The people of Summerside have helped me refine my communication by allowing me to stand up every Sunday, open God's Word, and teach about the power of the resurrection in our everyday lives.

Acknowledgments

I am eternally grateful to my wife, Heather, for years of living out the power of the resurrection and new life in our family and home. Apart from God's grace in salvation, you have been his greatest gift to me.

Abbreviations

Old Testament

Gen	Genesis
Ps/Pss	Psalms
Isa	Isaiah

New Testament

Matt	Matthew
Rom	Romans
1–2 Cor	1–2 Corinthians
Gal	Galatians
Phil	Philippians
1–2 Tim	1–2 Timothy
Jas	James
1–2 Pet	1–2 Peter
Rev	Revelation

1

Introduction

I THINK it was a Halloween party. At least I hope it was a Halloween party, because I distinctly remember being dressed up like Scorpion from *Mortal Kombat*. I didn't know many people there that night, and my wife was caught up in another conversation, so I did what I do best—head to the snacks. I stood around making small talk and connected with a guy I had encountered a few times throughout the city. His name is Dave.[1] We got chatting, and he asked me what I did for work. Now, I love being a pastor. It's what God has called me to do. But I do recognize that the times have passed when Reverends or "Holy Men" where held in high esteem. In the twenty-first century in Canada, being a pastor just isn't that cool.

So I told him what I did for a job. This led to a bunch of other questions, and from there the conversation really got going. I sensed an opening and began to ask him about his beliefs. After talking about the idea of "God" and if he exists, the Bible, the differences between my church and the Catholic church, the differences between Islam, Judaism, Buddhism, and Christianity, and a host of other topics (intense conversation for a Halloween

---

1. Obviously, his name wasn't Dave.

party, I know), I began to feel like we were treading water. He was all over the place, and in many ways, so was I. As we continued chatting and making a serious dent in the three-cheese dip, I remember thinking, *What can I offer him? What can I leave with him to encourage him to seriously consider Jesus?* Then it dawned on me—let's talk about the resurrection of Jesus.

For the next twenty minutes, or at least until I was getting dirty looks for eating all the snacks (and no, I didn't double dip), we talked about Jesus' resurrection. It was a tremendous opportunity, one of those rare encounters where there is real dialogue, openness, and a careful consideration of the opposing viewpoint. It was great. Unfortunately, Dave didn't fall to his knees, repent, and recognize Jesus as Lord. In fact, I don't see him around that much anymore, but I do try to pray for him whenever he comes to mind.

That night, I went home and remember having two thoughts. The *first* was that the resurrection of Jesus is tight. I mean, after sharing and talking about it with Dave and answering his questions, I was struck again by the evidence for Jesus' resurrection. I am so thankful for this. My *second* thought was that the Apostle Paul was right when he explained that the resurrection of Jesus from the dead really is the linchpin for our faith (1 Cor 15). If Jesus rose from the dead, then this whole Jesus-Bible-God-supernatural stuff is true.

It all comes back to the resurrection.

Are You Dave?

Maybe you're reading this and you're like Dave. Maybe you have a hundred questions, or a bunch of beliefs, or maybe exploring faith just seems so overwhelming. Maybe you're not sure about a lot of stuff, and the idea that you just need to "believe" seems like too much of an ask. Well, the good news is that it is. God doesn't call us to leap out into the dark or believe without evidence. He invites us to use the brain he has given us to think, question, learn, and grow.

Introduction

It's natural to have questions. After all, the idea that there is a God out there who made you, loves you, and has done everything needed to rescue you for himself can seem a bit far-fetched. The Bible is a big book and can seem daunting at first. Where do you start? Never mind the fact that Christianity around the world, and even in North America, seems to have a lot of differences from church to church or region to region. The hard part can be knowing where to start.

First off, reading the Bible is always a great place to start. For many people, reading something like one of the four Gospels proves to be not just interesting but also intriguing. The story of Jesus in the Gospels is pretty straightforward. Even today, pop-culture, music, and art often reference the events of the Gospels themselves. A lot of people are aware that Jesus was Jewish, that he taught, that he supposedly healed, and that he died on the cross. So if you read the Bible for the first time, while it's interesting, some of the content might not be that new to you. What people often find rather intriguing is what I call the "feel" of the Gospels. They aren't written like a fairy-tale. They read more like a biography. Many people, on first reading, are rather surprised by this. So starting with the Bible is a great place to begin.

The distinctions of Christian churches and denominations (think: Anglicans, Presbyterians, Brethren, Catholic, Baptists) can also seem hard to understand. I wanted to keep this book short, so while some of these denominations (and others) have some fairly significant differences, the vast majority of Christians are united around a number of specific, central tenants. Throughout history, Christians have gathered themselves together and written creeds and confessions. Many of these creeds are recognized by Christians of all stripes. So while the distinctions are important and worth exploring at some point, the central tenets of the Christian faith are well established.

One such example of this is what's commonly referred to as "The Apostle's Creed," or "The Creed." Written sometime around the fifth century in what is now modern-day France, this creed presents the core of Christian teaching.

> I believe in God, the Father almighty,
> creator of heaven and earth.
> And in Jesus Christ, his only Son, our Lord,
> who was conceived by the Holy Spirit
> born of the virgin Mary.
> suffered under Pontius Pilate,
> was crucified, died, and was buried;
> he descended to hell.
>   The third day he rose again from the dead.
> He ascended into heaven
> and is seated at the right hand of God the Father almighty.
> From there he will come to judge the living and the dead.
> I believe in the Holy Spirit,
> the holy catholic church,
> the communion of saints,
> the forgiveness of sins,
> the resurrection of the body,
> and life everlasting. Amen.

So again, while there are differences in Christian beliefs and practices around the world, the resurrection of Jesus forms the foundation of all Christianity. This means that it's the best place to begin your exploration. With that in mind, if you want to give it all a fair chance, rather than just dismissing it at a distance, it's going to involve two tasks. First, it will involve examining the resurrection, and secondly, to do that, you'll need to explore the Bible.

That's why I want to encourage you read through and think carefully about not just the text of this book but also the verses that are mentioned or referenced. If you have a Bible, the table of contents will serve you well. If you don't have a Bible, you can download any number of free apps, or simply google the reference.

There are any number of legitimate questions that people ask when they are considering exploring faith. Many of these can be difficult to understand at first—questions about good and evil, science and the Bible, the origins of sin, or Bible teachings on sexuality. But here's the thing: You don't want to put the cart before the horse. You don't want to start too far downstream or you won't understand how you've gotten there. So where should you start? With the Bible and the resurrection.

Introduction

More than an academic exercise, God wants you to experience him. This experience won't bypass your intellect; rather, it will involve your intellect. God invites our hearts to be opened to sense his presence and power. So if you are reading this and most of this is new, that's perfect. I'm not asking you to believe despite the evidence—I'm asking you to consider the possibility of believing, in part because of the evidence. That's why I'm writing this book.

Are You Already Convinced?

Maybe you're reading this and you're a tried-and-true follower of Christ. Maybe you have the t-shirt, bumper sticker, and can't bear to pass by one of those "Type Amen if you're not ashamed" Facebook posts (just so that we're all clear, I am pretty sure Jesus is OK if you just keep scrolling). If you're convinced that Jesus really did rise from the dead, that's great. My prayer is that this book will help you grow in that confidence and be better prepared to share this incredible news with whomever God puts in your path.

Those who follow Christ can expect to face trials, pushback, and a mix of sneers and jeers. In the Western world, Christianity is often viewed as a social faux pas—something that's only followed by narrow-minded bigots or the unenlightened. It's hard to follow Christ. Our hearts break for our brothers and sisters around the world who are suffering outright persecution and often violence or imprisonment. We weep for them. We pray for them. We stand amazed at their stories of endurance and faithfulness in the face of such opposition. But don't let that fool you into thinking that it's easy to follow Christ in the Western world. It's not. Like all believers throughout the ages, we wrestle with the flesh, we have an enemy who works against us, and we live in a fallen, broken world. Writing to a young pastor, the Apostle Paul explained, "In fact, everyone who wants to live a godly life in Christ Jesus will be persecuted" (2 Tim 3:12). This remains true today.

People outside of the Christian community often assume that believers themselves never question, doubt, wrestle with, or have second thoughts. If only that was the case. Some of the hardest questions about God, life, and the Bible that I've ever been asked have come from the lips of people who genuinely love Jesus and believe in him but have good and proper questions. As a pastor, I always encourage our people to think deeply, ask hard questions, and genuinely look for answers that satisfy. I encourage you to do the same. This doesn't mean that every single one of our specific questions about our past, our experiences, or our trauma will be simplistically answered, but it does mean that God's Word can and does offer us, "everything we need for life and godliness" (2 Pet 1:3). Since life is complex, the Bible is complex—not in a hard-to-understand or cryptic way, but in a nuanced, balanced, and works-in-real-life type of way.

It's natural for Christians to have questions and doubts. God doesn't call us to live our lives without asking questions. The problem is not in the questions we ask but in the way we seek for answers. If you have real questions or doubts, my encouragement to you is to actively seek answers that satisfy. Nothing is worse than having doubts and doing nothing about it.

When opposition, doubts, or struggle comes, and it will, you must have a deep and robust faith. Clichés, trite or simplistic explanations, a shallow faith—these things won't withstand the pressures that come. That's why I offer this book to you. I hope and pray that God, through his Spirit, will cause your roots to grow deep so that when the discouragement and opposition come, you'll stand firm. This is exactly what Paul is getting at when he writes,

> So then, just as you received Christ Jesus as Lord, continue to live your lives in him, rooted and built up in him, strengthened in the faith as you were taught, and overflowing with thankfulness.
> See to it that no one takes you captive through hollow and deceptive philosophy, which depends on human tradition and the elemental spiritual forces of this world rather than on Christ. (Col 2:6–8)

If the Christian faith in its entirety stands or falls on the resurrection of Jesus, what better way to be "rooted and built up" in your faith than by taking a serious look at this all-important event?

Introduction

So let me break it down: If Jesus really rose from the dead, it's all true. Every. Single. Part. All that the Bible records. All that Jesus claimed. Heaven, hell, life, death, hope, joy, peace—all these are real, and forgiveness and eternal joy are available.

If Jesus didn't rise from the dead, none of this is true. That means there is no reason to get out of bed on Sunday morning, read your Bible, pray, or feel guilty when you sin. Actually, the whole notion of "sin" becomes moot. It's a pointless discussion.

It's really an all or nothing equation. I mean, sure, even if Jesus didn't rise from the dead, he still said some nice things and challenged people to live their lives with love. But big deal. Lots of teachers throughout the years taught this. Buddha did. So did Muhammed. Every good parent I know teaches this to their kids: "Be kind. Do to others what you'd want them to do to you. Don't bite people." There have been many religious or inspirational teachers throughout the years—so why bother settling on Jesus as the one to follow, to give your life to? Again, I have to stress the point. It's all about the resurrection. No other religious leader, prophet, or holy person came back from the dead. Only Jesus did that. That's what makes Christianity different from other systems of belief. Niceness doesn't secure eternal life; Jesus does. Jesus accomplished this through his death and resurrection from the dead.

So let me ask you simply: Did it happen? Like, did it really/historically/actually happen? Was there really a man named Jesus who lived two thousand years ago, was crucified on a cross, and then, miraculously, three days later came back to life?

If Jesus really rose from the dead, it's all true.

If Jesus didn't rise from the dead, none of it is true.

You may have a thousand questions about life, faith, God, what comes after you die, why you're here on earth . . . those are good questions, and the answers will come. First, though, you must look at the foundation that all this rests upon: the resurrection of Jesus Christ from the dead.

2

The Non-Negotiables

Looking Back and Looking Ahead

As I'm sure you know, Easter Sunday is a big day for Christians. It's a day they specifically set aside every year to commemorate, reflect upon, and celebrate the resurrection of their King and Saviour, Jesus Christ. Without the resurrection of Jesus, there would be no such thing as Christianity

I'd like to take a few moments and invite you to look with me directly at this event—the resurrection. I'm not asking you to take a blind leap of faith into the unknown in following Jesus but to carefully consider the evidence and look at what the Bible records, as well as other alternative options offered to explain away this incredible occurrence.

Just before we jump into the historically established and generally accepted truths behind the life and ministry of Jesus, I want to take a minute and walk through the big picture of the Bible's story. Without a doubt, the resurrection of Jesus, from a theological standpoint, is the climax of the Bible. But a lot comes before, and much comes after that event. What comes before and what comes after helps us understand the reason and purpose of the resurrection. What comes after helps us understand the significance and real-world application of the resurrection. To start, let's go back.

Of the sixty-six books that make up the modern Bible, thirty-nine are what is often called the Old Testament. The Old Testament, written almost entirely in Hebrew, begins with the creation of the world and places special attention on the creation of humanity. It covers Israel's history until the coming of Jesus. The world is created perfect, but when sin is introduced, everything begins to fall apart. God's response, according to the Old Testament book of Genesis, is not to give up or walk away but to initiate the process of fixing all that is broken. God chooses a man named Abram to be the beginning of a new people who will follow him and join with him in enjoying the process of recreation. Abram (whose name is changed to Abraham) has sons, who have sons, who have sons. Eventually, his descendants end up in Egypt. After a period, his descendants, the nation of Israel, are enslaved. But God works through Moses to rescue them out of slavery. After a period of wandering through the desert, they enter the land of Canaan and begin to establish themselves. Throughout this time, God gives his people a religious system to follow, priests who serve, and a temple in which to worship him. Eventually, Israel's kings fail to lead well, and as a result, the nation is conquered and the people are dragged off into exile.

Even in exile, God isn't done with his people. He sends prophets, leaders, and teachers to guide his people back from exile to their home in Israel. Then the Old Testament ends. But it doesn't end with just a sense of joy or relief at being gathered back to Israel; it ends with a sense of anticipation. Through the prophets he sent, God explained that he would fulfill all his promises to Israel, and that the best was still to come.

The New Testament, written in Greek, basically begins with the birth of Jesus. Sure, there's a bit more background, genealogical information, and context, but Jesus' earthly origins are the starting point. The four Gospels—Matthew, Mark, Luke, and John—introduce us to their main character, Jesus, and give information, accounts, and stories about his life, ministry, and teachings. Each of the four Gospels give significant time and attention to his death by crucifixion. Jesus is then raised from the dead and commissions his disciples to go out into the whole world and proclaim his victory over death, sin, and evil. But after the four Gospels, you have twenty-three more books basically covering his disciples, the early church, and doing just as he commanded.

As his followers began to share the news of his life, death, and resurrection, many more people became followers of Jesus. As this happened, churches were formed throughout the Roman Empire. Many of the books of the New Testament are written by Jesus' Apostles to specific churches in various cities or individuals throughout the empire.

There is so much more that could be said about both the Old Testament and the New. But for now, simply gaining a sense of the big picture of the Bible is sufficient. The Old Testament reveals the reason *why* Jesus had to die on the cross. The Gospels reveal how it all happened and that Jesus didn't stay dead. The rest of the New Testament reveals the transformative power of the Good News of all that Jesus did and accomplished and how that very message changed the world.

Here we are today, nearly two thousand years later, and the message of the death and resurrection of Jesus has transformed the world. It is estimated that there are over two billion Christians world-wide. Far from being a Western religion, Christianity is thriving throughout the developing world in diverse regions and people groups.

What We Know from History

That Jesus existed is almost universally recognized by scholars. Whether they are Christian scholars who follow Jesus, or agnostics who don't buy the message of the Bible at all, reputable scholars accept that Jesus was a real historical figure. For example, John Dominic Crossan, a scholar known for his overtly skeptical and critical positions about the New Testament, offers his thoughts:

The Non-Negotiables

"I conclude that Jesus was an actual, factual, historical figure and not a metaphorical, symbolic, or parabolic invention by his first-century Jewish contemporaries."[1]

Another voice to add to this point is Bart Ehrman. Ehrman is best known as an apologist (defender) of unorthodox and highly critical views of Christianity. While he writes and speaks extensively in the hopes—it seems—of "de-converting" people from Christianity, his work as a scholar has led him to explain that there really is no scholarly debate about Jesus' existence. Yes, you may come across blog posts or angry comments explaining that Jesus is a myth, but in response to these "authors," Ehrman writes,

> I should say at the outset that none of this literature is written by scholars trained in New Testament or early Christian studies teaching at the major, or even the minor, accredited theological seminaries, divinity schools, universities, or colleges of North America or Europe (or anywhere else in the world). Of the thousands of scholars of early Christianity who do teach at such schools, none of them, to my knowledge, has any doubts that Jesus existed. But a whole body of literature out there, some of it highly intelligent and well informed, makes this case.[2]

What we know is that there was a man named Jesus, from Nazareth, who was born about two thousand years ago. He was baptized in the Jordan River, gathered followers, and was a great teacher. This Jesus of Nazareth, history records, ultimately died on a Roman cross. And here's the final point that is widely accepted: Jesus' disciples *actually believed* that he rose from the dead. This is key. It's not simply a case that they claimed he had risen but that they believed he did. One New Testament scholar goes so far as to say, "Those scholars who are unable to believe in an actual resurrection of Jesus admit that the disciples believed it."[3]

Let's work through some of these statements, because despite what you may read in comment sections on YouTube, or the

---

1. Corssan, *The Power of Parable*, 251.
2. Ehrman, *Did Jesus Exist?*, 2.
3. Ladd, *Theology*, 320.

debates you get pulled into on Facebook, this point—the historicity of Jesus—is a settled issue. How do we arrive at this conclusion? By looking at the historical data. Let me make five points about the data that we have:

Jesus and His Followers Are Mentioned outside of the Bible

Even if someone is skeptical of the truthfulness of the Bible and excludes it from the conversation, Jesus' existence is still well supported from history. Gary Habermas, a prominent New Testament scholar and historian, in his helpful book, *The Historical Jesus*, presents a number of significant references to Jesus and the events of the Gospels in addition to what we find in the Bible. He offers, among others, the following:

- Cornelius Tacitus (ca. 55–120 CE). Tacitus, a famous Roman historian, wrote towards the end of the first century into the beginning of the second. His writings cover the Roman Empire and span the rule of emperors. In his *Annals*, or what remains of it, he references the early Christian movement in Rome in the year 55–65 CE. He writes that Christians derived their name from their founder, Christ; that Jesus was put to death by Pilate; and that after Jesus' death, his "teachings" broke out again.[4]

- Suetonius (writing in the early second century about events in the first century), another Roman historian, refers to some of the troublemakers in Rome as being Jewish individuals who followed "Chrestus."[5] Many historians explain this as an alternative way to spell *Christ*.[6] He also (as did Tacitus) mentions the great fire in Rome and that "Christians" were behind it.

---

4. For a more detailed engagement with Tacticus' work, see: Habermas, *The Historical Jesus*, 187–191.
5. Suetonius, *Claudius*, 25.
6. Bruce, *New Testament History*, 297–98.

The Non-Negotiables

- Josephus (born ca. 37 CE) was a Jewish historian who mentioned Jesus on two occasions.[7] Though one of these references is debated, since it's an unusually positive comment regarding Jesus coming from a former Pharisee and skeptic, most historians agree that, in the very least, he was aware of Jesus and chose to mention him in his historical treatise.[8]

There are many other evidences, references, or records from the first two centuries demonstrating that the Jesus of the Bible was a real person who lived in Jerusalem in the first century. The books mentioned by Habermas and Licona provide a much more detailed and critical interaction with these ancient historians. But let's be clear, the point stands that Jesus is mentioned in literature outside of the Bible.

If you deny the historical existence of Jesus of Nazareth, then pretty much any historical figure can be explained away. If Jesus wasn't real, how do you have confidence that anyone, from Alexander the Great to George Washington, was real? If, despite all the evidence that we have, you still don't believe that Jesus existed, how can you believe anyone existed before 1900?

The New Testament Is Not a Singular Book but a Collection of Different Books by Different Authors

Someone may say, "Show me a source outside the Bible that talks about Jesus." Well, we can do that, but the question itself is flawed. In this type of question, the Bible is assumed to be one source, like a book that mentions Jesus several times. But that's not the case.

The Bible is a library of books. It was written in different times by different people. Think about the New Testament Gospels—Matthew, Mark, Luke, John. These are four *different* sources that record the life, ministry, death, and resurrection of Jesus. When you add to this the letters written by Paul, Peter, James, Jude, and the writer of Hebrews—all of which either mention, build on, or

---

7. Josephus, *Antiquities*, 20:200.
8. See Habermas, *The Historical Jesus*, 192–94.

assume the truth that is found in the Gospels—it's clear that we're talking about something much more dynamic than one source. These are all different sources that say, essentially, the same thing. This isn't one person in the witness stand; this is a whole group of people offering their assessment. That they have been collected and combined to form the New Testament doesn't minimize that they are, in fact, many sources. And these sources agree: Jesus lived, taught, healed, died, and rose again.

There are far fewer sources, written within two hundred years, about Genghis Kahn than there are written about Jesus. The early Christians, those that came after the Apostles, wrote commentaries, sermons, and theological treatises in which they quoted the New Testament documents consistently and constantly.

The New Testament Gospels and Letters Were Written Near to the Time of the Events They Record

Sometimes, people will argue against the point made above. They'll argue that the New Testament was likely written hundreds of years after the events, so even if they all agreed about Jesus, they were essentially making it up or recording rumors of rumors, so we really can't take them seriously as a source. After all, we've all seen how time can corrupt even a simple message and that the more a story is shared and then reshaped, the likelier some form of corruption has occurred—or at least that's how the argument goes.

But it's not that simple. Many of the New Testament books were written within a few decades of Jesus' life, death, and resurrection. For example, the Gospel of Mark, presumably the first Gospel written, is usually dated to around 45–60 CE, with some scholars contending it could have been written as early as the late thirties CE.[9] Likewise, Paul's letter to the Galatians is dated to around 50 CE.[10] The majority of the New Testament books were written in

---

9. Crossley, *The Date of Mark's Gospel: Insights from the Law in Earliest Christianity*.

10. Polhill, *Paul and his Letters*, 138.

The Non-Negotiables

the fifties and sixties, with some of John's writings rounding out the timeline, being composed, most likely, in the nineties.

An example of this is found in 1 Corinthians 15. In this chapter, the Apostle Paul is talking about the resurrection to the small, troubled church in the city of Corinth. He recounts the resurrection events and then adds this line regarding the various witnesses, "many of whom are still living" (1 Cor 15:6). The point here is that these Christians in Corinth could still access those who witnessed the literal resurrection of Jesus from the dead. Clearly, this wasn't hundreds of years after the events. People, generally speaking, didn't live that long in the ancient world!

What this all means is that we're not talking about decades upon decades of oral transmission. At the time of the writing of the New Testament Gospels, many of the original eyewitnesses would still have been living. The "telephone game" understanding of the New Testament writings does not do justice to the historical reality of their composition.

The "Autographs" (Original Gospels/Letters) Would Have Been Prized, Protected, and Likely Lasted for Many Years, Allowing New Copies to Be Compared to These Originals

This is a bit of a complex issue, so I'll explain it as clearly as I can. In the Ancient World, libraries were rather common. For example, in Rome during the reign of Caesar Augustus, a number of libraries were built.[11] Because books ("codices" is the technical term), manuscripts, and letters were expensive and time consuming to create, they were often prized and protected. Archaeologists, however, often uncover garbage in the areas that served as ancient cities' dumps: pot shards, paper fragments, and inscriptions.[12]

Larger works and more important works were often housed in something like a library. The question then follows: How long

---

11. Dix and Houston, "Public Libraries in the City of Rome."
12. Well, where do your grocery lists, notes of, "I'll be back in twenty," or your children's coloring often end up? In the garbage!

did some of these works last? Imagine that someone in the Ancient World writes a *Roman-Times* best seller—some philosophy tract or something. It would have been preserved and protected for a long time. Scholars have noted that these original works were often preserved between 150 and 500 years.[13] What this means is that any subsequent copy or edition didn't exist in a vacuum. If someone had a copy that was made one or two hundred years later, they likely would have still been able to check and compare to the original that remained in circulation.

What does this mean for the New Testament? Well, since the early church recognized the authority of the apostles, they would have protected and prized the original works. If someone made a copy of the original, the two could be compared. Imagine someone in the third century copying down the book of Mark. Let's say that the person is a bit sloppy, careless, and wants to spice it up a bit (make Jesus a ten-foot tall, fire-breathing, laser-beam-eyed man). The original, written by Mark, would still have been around and in the possession of the early church leadership. This means that the original works of the New Testament could have been guiding, correcting, and ensuring the accuracy of copies for many, many years.

This concept counters the whole "copy of a copy of a copy" thought. It's not as if a copy was made, the original destroyed, then another copy made, and the first copy destroyed. The originals would have been in possession of the church for a significant amount of time and, therefore, helped prevent against error and inaccuracies.[14]

Jesus' Followers Believed the Tomb Was Empty

Regardless of how you might explain the resurrection event, this much is clear: the disciples of Jesus really believed the tomb was empty. The early church was birthed from this belief. Jesus'

---

13. Evans, *Jesus and His World*, 75.
14. Evans, *Jesus and His World*, 76.

The Non-Negotiables

disciples went out from Jerusalem and began to proclaim that Jesus was raised from the dead. It's possible to make the case that they were mistaken, but the point remains that it was their conviction, their sincere belief that he was raised from the dead.

The Apostle Peter was one of Jesus' closest friends. He witnessed first-hand Jesus' life and ministry. He also had a front row seat to Jesus' trial and crucifixion (Luke 22:54–62). What's fascinating is that Peter, when witnessing the trial and crucifixion, began to struggle and ended up "denying" Jesus. This infamous account is recorded in detail and doesn't place Peter in a very positive light. Despite Peter's struggle, after witnessing the resurrection, he becomes a leader in spreading the Good News of Jesus. Peter, in his letter, writes,

> Blessed be the God and Father of our Lord Jesus Christ! According to his great mercy, he has caused us to be born again to a living hope through the resurrection of Jesus Christ from the dead (1 Pet 1:3)

After all his personal struggles and after witnessing the events of Jesus' trial, death, and resurrection, Peter ends up believing that Jesus' tomb was empty, that he had been raised from the dead.

In addition to the example of Peter, you can read the Gospels, particularly Matthew, Luke, and John. In each of these, Jesus' followers are presented as believing that the tomb was in fact empty. In Matthew, Mary Magdalene and "the other Mary"—female disciples of Jesus—see the empty tomb and meet the resurrected Jesus (Matt 28:1–10) In Luke, the women actually enter the tomb, look around, and note that the body is gone (Luke 24:1–12). What's especially interesting about Luke's account is how he presents the disciples' response to the claim from the women that the tomb was empty. Luke writes, "but they did not believe the women, because their words seemed to them like nonsense" (Luke 24:11). Clearly, the disciples weren't desperately looking for a reason to believe, thus disengaging their discernment and rationality. They didn't believe because the idea of someone being raised from the dead *is* hard to believe! Luke goes on to record that in hearing this news,

Peter ran to the tomb for himself to check (Luke 24:12). Just like the women, Peter went into the tomb to check on the body.

In the Gospel accounts, the disciples not only witness an empty tomb but see the resurrected Jesus. This is important. One without the other could much more easily be explained away than both together. If the disciples merely found the tomb empty, there are any number of explanations for such an event. If they merely claimed to have seen Jesus, but the body was actually still in the tomb, then we'd be talking about a mystical or metaphorical resurrection. Both together, as we find in the Gospels, are hard to explain away.

Let me recap what we've covered. Jesus existed. That much is beyond dispute. He lived, taught, made some incredible claims, and was crucified on a cross in Jerusalem. His followers genuinely believed that he rose from the dead after his crucifixion. So, the question is this: How do we make sense of the claims of his followers that Jesus was resurrected? Well, I'd like to share with you some of the competing theories people propose for the resurrection.

3

Alternative Explanations for the Resurrection

Recently, a friend told me about a rather uncomfortable event that took place a few years ago. He had just finished his undergrad at Bible college. For all intents and purposes, in the eyes of his extended family, he was a full-fledged priest. He went to the hospital to visit an elderly, distant aunt. As the family gathered around her bed, a member of her immediate family asked him to pray for her. For a young guy without a lot of experience, in front of non-Christian family members, this was a bit daunting. Nevertheless, looking to be a comfort to the family and hoping to have a positive impact, he took hold of his great aunt's hand and began praying. With all heads bowed and his eyes closed, he prayed that God would comfort the family and that his great aunt would find peace and experience God's presence. He went on to pray that, if it was God's will, she'd be healed and restored. He said "amen," got a few uncomfortable glances from the family, and left the room.

A minute later, his mom, who is also a believer, met him in the hallway. She looked at him wide-eyed and said something that explained the reason for the odd looks he'd received from the extended family. His great aunt had died twenty minutes before he came into the room! The hand he was holding and the prayers for healing he had offered were offered for someone who had already passed away. He had no idea. No one had told him. He had accidently prayed for healing for a dead person. He had inadvertently prayed for a resurrection.

Suddenly, the odd looks he'd received after he prayed made sense. People who have been dead for twenty minutes generally stay that way. You don't need to be a medical doctor to know this.

Incredibly, Jesus' followers claimed that he did in fact do what is generally understood to be impossible—he rose from the dead. So how do people explain away these claims? There are a number of "explanations" ranging from serious to, well, less serious. Supposing you don't believe that aliens abducted Jesus, or that he had a secret twin brother or doppelgänger, here are a few of the more common and popular theories.

The Swoon Theory

Here's one way to explain the resurrection. Jesus was crucified on a cross, but he didn't actually die. He merely passed out from blood loss and trauma. He was taken down from the cross and placed in a cold tomb. After some time in that cold tomb, the brisk air revived him, and he left the tomb to go see his disciples. Upon seeing Jesus, the disciples believed and declared that he had been resurrected. He wasn't actually resurrected because he didn't really die. We've all heard crazy stories about people surviving accidents, falls, or trauma wherein 99.9 percent of the time it results in death. Jesus was just an outlier, an exception.

These types of exceptions do occur. For an example of this, you can think of the movie *The Revenant,* starring Leonardo DiCaprio. While the writers of the movie took some creative liberties, the story itself (including the terrifying bear mauling) is based on a true story. After being grievously injured by the mother bear, Hugh Glass was incapacitated and thought to be near death. The two men who stayed behind to tend to him thought his chances

Alternative Explanations for the Resurrection

were minimal, so eventually, they left him to die alone. According to the biographers, Glass chose to forgive the men who left him rather than kill them, as the movies portrayed. But then again, I get it. We all love a little bit of revenge and retribution in film. In the end, somehow and against all odds, Glass survived. I mean, surely, if someone can survive a bear attack, they can survive crucifixion, right?

Let's think about this for a second.

First of all, you don't survive crucifixion. The Romans, the ones who crucified Jesus on the cross—this wasn't their first kick at the can. They weren't thinking: *Okay, let's try this crucifixion thing out. Now, where do the nails go? How do we do this?* No, the Romans were experts at crucifixion and knew exactly what they were doing. They had perfected it. When you read the Bible's account of the crucifixion, you see that they specifically checked to see if Jesus was, in fact, dead.[1] Can you imagine if you were the Roman centurion whose one job was to kill somebody on a cross and you messed it up? You would have found yourself right up there being crucified in the next round. Make no mistake, these trained soldiers knew what they were doing. Playing dead may work in a bear attack, but with trained Roman centurions, it's not a viable option.

But let's imagine that, somehow, as impossible as it would be, the centurion guard did, in fact, miss the mark, and Jesus was placed in the tomb alive but unconscious, and he eventually came to. We've still got a problem. I don't know if you work out and have ever tried to do some dead-lifts or CrossFit with holes in your hands and feet and a gaping wound in your side, but it's impossible. The entrance to Jesus' tomb was sealed by a giant boulder (Matt 27:60; Luke 24:2), and he was not going to be setting personal lift records after suffering through such a terrible ordeal. It doesn't make sense. How could he possibly survive, let alone find

---

1. See: John 19:23–37, specifically verses 33–34: "But when they came to Jesus and found that he was already dead, they did not break his legs. Instead, one of the soldiers pierced Jesus' side with a spear, bringing a sudden flow of blood and water."

the strength (remember—no food or water for three days) to roll the stone away from the tomb's entrance?

Not only did Jesus appear to his disciples, but he also traveled quite a distance after his resurrection. In Matthew's account, Jesus appears to the two Marys and tells them to go to Galilee (Matt 28:10). Jesus then appears to his followers in the area he had sent them to (Matt 28:16). Here's why this is important. Jesus was crucified in Jerusalem. He appears to his disciples in Galilee, and there teaches them more about what has happened. Jerusalem is just under eighty miles (130 kilometers) from Galilee. If Jesus merely swooned on the cross, somehow surviving crucifixion, that's quite the trek to make after suffering a life-threatening injury like that. That's easily three or four long days of hard hiking over difficult terrain. Most of us couldn't walk that distance even at the best of times, let alone with gaping flesh wounds, blood loss, and extreme pain. Never mind the fact that hiking with newly acquired shoes is hard enough, to say nothing about newly acquired nail holes in those same feet!

Again, if he somehow, after three days of blood loss, extreme trauma, and no food or water, makes it to the lodging where the disciples are, and they see him standing there with festering wounds, clearly on the verge of death, they would not say: "It's a miracle! He's been raised from the dead!" They'd look at him and, in absolute astonishment, say: "Wow, he survived somehow!" There's a big difference between thinking someone survived versus someone having been raised from the dead. The disciples weren't stupid. They were hard men living in a day and age when life was hard. They had seen people hurt and injured before. They saw him and concluded that he really was raised from the dead.

Let's be honest—this whole Swoon Theory does not hold up.

Mass Hallucination

Here's one for the psychedelics or hallucinogens crowd. The disciples thought Jesus was raised from the dead because, well, they were "tripping."

Alternative Explanations for the Resurrection

Michael Goulder is a well-known scholar and historian. He argues that the disciples, because of their grief, brokenness, and sadness at Jesus' death after they'd invested years following him, suffered some form of mass hallucination.[2] They mistakenly believed that they saw the resurrected Jesus. They were distraught, saddened, and discouraged, and because of this and the very real risks they faced from further persecution, they experienced a vision of Jesus—that he was raised from the dead.

This explanation of the resurrection has a few problems, apart from the fact that LSD wasn't invented until 1938 by a Swiss chemist. To be sure, hallucinations, whether induced by chemicals or mental health issues, are present in human experience. In 2001, Russel Crowe portrayed John Nash, an award-winning mathematician. Based on a true story, the movie presents Nash's paranoid schizophrenia and delusions in such a way that the viewer doesn't notice the hallucinations until the mid-point of the story. The director, Ron Howard, presents the delusions in such striking and vivid ways that it's completely understandable why Nash truly does believe his experiences are real. Was this the case with the disciples?

Michael Licona, in his excellent book on the resurrection, explains the problems with Goulder's view.[3] First, Licona points out that the American Psychological Association (APA) notes that 15 percent of people will suffer some form of hallucination in their life. Oftentimes, these hallucinations can be auditory (thinking you hear something), visual (thinking you see something), or sensory (believing you are sensing something or someone). Only about 15 percent of the population will experience something akin to this, and very rarely do these hallucinations feature multiple groupings of senses. Apparently, the older you are, the more prone you are to these types of hallucinations.

Yet when you read the New Testament, you'll see that it's not fifteen percent of people who say something like: "I saw this quick

---

2. Goulder, "The Baseless Fabric of a Vision," in *Resurrection Reconsidered*, ed. Gavin D'Costa.
3. Licona, *The Resurrection of Jesus*, 479–495.

glimpse of something" or "I thought I heard Jesus' voice when I was praying" or even "I think I sense Jesus with us now." When you read the New Testament, you see that his disciples, and many others, claimed to have seen Jesus, heard him, touched him, and ate with him. To say that this is a mass hallucination is, again, difficult to accept, as nothing akin to this has ever happened in history—and that's the whole point: The resurrection of Jesus Christ from the dead is miraculous.

The Disciples Stole the Body

What if, upon seeing their leader executed, the disciples began to scramble and came up with a plan? Maybe they decided that they had invested too much in this movement to give up now, so they conspired together, came in under the cover of darkness, and stole Jesus' body. This was perhaps the earliest theory used to explain away the resurrection (Matt 28:12–14).

Okay, now this theory makes sense. But we must ask *why* the disciples would have done that. If you read the New Testament and other historical accounts, you'll see that the disciples went to their deaths proclaiming that Jesus really was raised from the dead. It's not like this was a power move on their part and that somehow, by claiming that Jesus was raised from the dead, their lives improved.

None of them had private jets, lots of ladies, incredible power and influence in the world, or were living the high-life with champagne and caviar. You can read about their experience. They were hunted. They were hated. They were rounded up like common criminals with all but one of them dying for their belief that Jesus was indeed raised to life. You would think that at some point, if it was just a made-up farce, at least one of them would have said: "Okay, this has gone too far. We've had our fun, but I'm not dying for this lie." Yet they were all willing to die proclaiming that Jesus had literally risen from the dead. Who would make up a story that results in their own death? Craig Keener makes a solid point:

Alternative Explanations for the Resurrection

"People of course die regularly for values that are false; they do *not*, however, ordinarily voluntarily for what they *believe* is false."[4]

One guy who gets this is Chuck Colson. He served as part of the troubled Richard Nixon administration in the 1970s. As Special Counsel, he was known as President Nixon's "hatchet man." In 1974, he pleaded guilty to obstruction of justice and served time in prison for his role in the infamous Watergate scandal. After becoming a Christian, Colson went on to write and speak about the Christian faith and the resurrection of Jesus. On this, he explained:

> "Here were the 10 most powerful men in the United States. With all that power, and we couldn't contain a lie for two weeks . . . Take it from one who was involved in conspiracy, who saw the frailty of man firsthand. There is no way the 11 apostles, who were with Jesus at the time of the resurrection, could ever have gone around for 40 years proclaiming Jesus' resurrection unless it were true."[5]

In the words of Blaise Pascal, "I prefer to believe those writers who get their throats cut for what they write."[6]

The story of Thomas in John 20 is worth mentioning here. Thomas was one of Jesus' original disciples. When word began to spread among the disciples that Jesus was raised from the dead, not all of them bought it. Thomas said,

> Now Thomas (also known as Didymus), one of the Twelve, was not with the disciples when Jesus came. So the other disciples told him, "We have seen the Lord!" But he said to them, "Unless I see the nail marks in his hands and put my finger where the nails were, and put my hand into his side, I will not believe." (John 20:24–25)

Thomas had to personally *see* Jesus before he was willing to believe. It wasn't some elaborate hoax cooked up by devoted followers wishing to pursue some form of gain. It was miraculous,

---

4. Keener, *The Historical Jesus of the Gospels*, 342.
5. Hyer, "Colson Preaches," lines 6–15.
6. As quoted by: Moriarty, *Pascal*, 320.

incredible, and hard to believe. It took seeing for Thomas to believe, which is exactly what happened in the following verses,

> A week later his disciples were in the house again, and Thomas was with them. Though the doors were locked, Jesus came and stood among them and said, "Peace be with you!" Then he said to Thomas, "Put your finger here; see my hands. Reach out your hand and put it into my side. Stop doubting and believe." Thomas said to him, "My Lord and my God!" (John 20:26–28)

The disciples believed because they saw Jesus resurrected from the dead.

The Disciples Went to the Wrong Tomb

Sometimes mistakes happen. Paul Drecksler, a thirty-seven-year-old man, had just endured an arduous journey back from Ecuador, landing in Miami to attend a friend's wedding.[7] He rented an Airbnb, was communicating with the host, and followed the instructions he was given. As the host requested, he went in through the gate, let himself into the home, closed the door quickly to avoid letting the dog out, found the bedroom, and collapsed in exhaustion. Early the next morning, he heard a knock on the door and woke to someone asking him what he was doing. He calmy explained that this was his rental unit, and that he had followed all instructions. The only problem was that he was supposed to be next door! Both houses had the same gate location, a dog inside the house, and an unlocked door. Thankfully, he and the homeowner were quickly able to understand that this was an honest mistake. But here's the point: mistakes do happen.

What if this is what happened to the disciples? They must have been exhausted. Their leader and teacher had just been executed. They were obviously distressed and heartbroken at what had happened. Maybe when the women went to the tomb they made a critical error: they went to the wrong tomb. Maybe if they

---

7. Goodyear, "He thought he was crashing at his Airbnb."

Alternative Explanations for the Resurrection

had just looked "next door," they would have found the correct tomb, but as it was, they found the tomb empty and ran off to tell the disciples. From there the excitement grew, and more than likely, no one bothered to double check that they had the right tomb.

There are two primary issues with this theory. To understand them, you have to look back at the resurrection accounts as recorded in the Gospels. While it is true that oftentimes criminals who were crucified were left on the cross to rot and be consumed by birds or wild dogs after their death, this was not the case in Jesus' death. In Matthew 27:57–61, we read,

> As evening approached, there came a rich man from Arimathea, named Joseph, who had himself become a disciple of Jesus. Going to Pilate, he asked for Jesus' body, and Pilate ordered that it be given to him. Joseph took the body, wrapped it in a clean linen cloth, and placed it in his own new tomb that he had cut out of the rock. He rolled a big stone in front of the entrance to the tomb and went away. Mary Magdalene and the other Mary were sitting there opposite the tomb.

Now notice a few things here. First of all, the man introduced here, Joseph of Arimathea, was more than likely an intelligent and well-trained individual. He was a member of the Sanhedrin council—the very group that voted in agreement to have Jesus crucified. Luke explains that Joseph did not in fact join with the other members of the Sanhedrin in condemning Jesus to die (Luke 23:50, 51). Joseph, we're told, was a "rich man," and as a man of means, he had a tomb purchased and ready to use. It was a tomb he'd cut himself—or more likely paid to have it done—so it had never been used before. As a follower of Jesus, he had his teacher's body buried in his own tomb that he had prepared.

Think about it. A rich man chose a tomb, had work done on it, and brought Jesus to that very tomb. I have a hard time believing that after all the time, energy, and money he sunk into preparing this tomb for himself, he forgot which tomb was his. Not only that, but he went to the tomb with two women—the same two women who were the first two eyewitnesses. That's three people who had

27

been to the tomb before the resurrection—one of which, the owner, had more than likely been there a number of times. What are the odds that all three made the same mistake?

Secondly, there is an even bigger problem with the theory that the disciples made a glaring mistake. The early church message and the spread of Christianity was not based on an empty tomb alone but on the empty tomb *and* seeing and speaking with the resurrected Jesus. If there were no post-resurrection appearances by Jesus, then this theory could make sense. But the disciples clearly believed that they not only had the right tomb, and that it was empty, but that they also saw the resurrected Jesus. The idea that it was all a grand mistake makes sense only on a surface reading, when you avoid the specific evidence and logic found in the source material.

Evaluating Explanations

As you can see, there aren't a lot of great explanations for the resurrection event apart from what the Bible records. Do you really think that something unprecedented like mass group hallucinations or Jesus somehow surviving crucifixion is truthfully an airtight explanation? The problem with the resurrection for skeptics and doubters is that it's easy to throw out alternative explanations from a distance. But once you get closer and think through the implications and arguments that these views give, it becomes harder and harder to take them seriously. Jesus' disciples actually believed he rose from the dead. This is key.

Even if you are skeptical and having a hard time believing it, my encouragement is to think carefully about an alternative explanation. If the resurrection didn't happen—literally and physically—thus launching the early church out into the world with conviction, passion, and excitement, then how did it all start? If Jesus wasn't raised from the dead, why did the disciples say that he was? If this was a made-up story, why were his followers willing to die for their beliefs? If Jesus somehow survived crucifixion, how did he roll the stone away, walk two-marathons worth of distance,

Alternative Explanations for the Resurrection

show up and be welcomed by his followers as someone who had conquered death rather than just survived it?

The message of the resurrection has, without a doubt, changed the world forever. If you don't think that it's true, my challenge to you is to locate an explanation that does better justice to the selected evidence presented here. If you have a better answer to the historical evidence, great. If not, dig a bit deeper and be open to the possibility that maybe Jesus' early followers were telling the truth. That is where we turn our attention to next—the evidence itself.

4

Evidence for the Resurrection

So if the disciples weren't strung out on LSD and didn't contrive some elaborate lie that resulted in their deaths, let's look at what the Gospels record and evaluate their explanation of what happened. We'll start with the first book of the New Testament, the Gospel of Matthew. Rather than simply taking my word for it, or that of some other pastor, priest, or spiritual guru, look at the actual eyewitness accounts and see how these individuals understood what happened.

The book of Matthew begins the resurrection account like this:

> After the sabbath, at dawn, on the first day of the week, Mary Magdalene and the other Mary went up to look at the tomb. There was a violent earthquake for an angel of the Lord came down from heaven and, going to the tomb, rolled back the stone and sat on it. His appearance was like lightening and his clothes were white as snow. The guards were so afraid of him that they shook and became like dead men. The angels said to the women 'Do not be afraid for I know you are looking for Jesus who was crucified. He is not here, he is risen just as he said. Come and see the place where they lay him. Then

Evidence for the Resurrection

go quickly and tell his disciples he has risen from the dead and is going ahead of you into Galilee. There you will see him. Now I have told you.' So the women hurried away from the tomb, afraid yet filled with joy and ran to tell the disciples. Suddenly, Jesus met them. 'Greetings', he said. They came to him and they clasped his feet and worshiped him. And then Jesus said to them 'Do not be afraid. Go and tell my brothers to go to Galilee. There they will see me.' (Matt 28:1–10)

It's a powerful account to read, but historically something significant happens here. To be fair, it may not mean much to you and me in the twenty-first century, living in a Western context, but this is rather enlightening.

Evidence 1: Credible Witnesses Because They Were Not "Credible"

Who are the first witnesses of the resurrection? Two women.

This doesn't mean much to us, but if you go back to the Greco-Roman way of thinking, as well as even some Jewish thinking of the time, you'll see that the testimony of women was not highly esteemed. In fact, in much of the Jewish literature of the day, such as Rosh Hoshana 1:8, you'll see that the testimony of a woman is worth less than that of a thief's—essentially half that of a man's. There are dozens of interpersonal letters, as well as historical records, from this time period that contain very unflattering things about the testimony and trustworthiness of women. Obviously, this was wrong, but think about what this means.

If you and I were to get together and make up a story to build our own religion or following, why would we base that story on the witness and testimony of two individuals who were not highly esteemed? Imagine if we hatched a scheme to dupe people. As we were planning our elaborate ruse, do you really think that we'd land on two criminals, perjurers, or thieves as our star witnesses? Absolutely not. If it was all a lie, we'd want to create an account in which reliable witnesses were used to press our case.

31

In Matthew, just one chapter before this, we're introduced to a man, Joseph of Arimathea (Matt 27:57). He was a well-respected individual who was also a follower of Jesus and offered Jesus his own tomb. As an influential, religious, and educated man, he would be just the right type of individual on which to base your credibility. So again, I ask you, why do the Gospel writers point to two women as the first witnesses?

Simply because that's what actually happened.

All four gospels record that women were the first witnesses of the resurrection of Jesus. There are even ancient writers who pointed this out to Christians as a reason to not accept this as credible evidence.[1] For many ancient readers, this did, in fact, detract from the validity of the account, yet it's the evidence offered—because it's what actually happened.

Evidence 2: "Go Ahead, Fact Check Me"

Let me offer you another key piece of evidence. We find this in 1 Corinthians 15, where the apostle Paul is writing.

> Now brothers and sisters, I want to remind you of the gospel that I preach to you, on which you have received and on which you have taken your stand. By this gospel you are saved for what I received I passed onto you as a first importance, that Christ died for our sins according to the Scriptures, that he was buried and that he was raised on the third day according to the Scriptures, and that he appeared to Cephus and then to the twelve. After that, he appeared to more than five hundred of the brothers and sisters at the same time, many of whom are still living though some have fallen asleep. Then he appeared to James, then to the apostles, and last of all, he appeared to me." (1 Cor 15:1–8)

This is a famous testimony of the resurrection, and there are three things that I think are important to notice here. Think about

---

1. See, for example, the list provided by Keener, *The Historical Jesus of the Gospels*, note 7, 579.

Evidence for the Resurrection

this wording: "the five hundred witnesses, many of whom are still living." If I were making up a story, I wouldn't give you the information you'd need to fact check me. Yet that's exactly what Paul does in this passage of scripture. He says there are five hundred witnesses to the resurrection, and many of them are still living! He's encouraging readers to go talk to these witnesses, to check out the evidence for themselves. If all of this was just a conspiracy, Paul would not have offered this encouragement. He would have kept the details ambiguous, holding his readers at arm's length. Once again, the reason Paul has the confidence to do this is because the account he offers is true, leaving no reason to camouflage or protect the specifics of the story.

Imagine yourself sitting in a courtroom. The prosecution calls a witness, and the testimony is that such-and-such happened. Now imagine that there were twelve witnesses called who all said the same thing. That would bolster the case, to be sure! Now imagine that there were not just twelve, but five hundred witnesses called to the stand. At some point, you'd have to accept that if there are that many eyewitnesses, we should seriously consider that the events happened as described.

Why would Paul leave himself open to this type of scrutiny? Imagine someone applying for a new job. To impress the perspective employer, they decide to lie on their resume. They claim all manner of educational degrees, some fantastic work experience, and a number of impressive references (Elon Musk, a few former presidents, and Lebron James). Now imagine after each bold-faced-lie, they provided detailed contact information for the school, businesses, and people mentioned. What would happen? The first phone call or email from the employer checking into the person's claims would reveal the truth—it's all a big lie. It would be much easier for a person to make these types of claims but do so in such a way that makes it hard for the employer to get to the truth. It's the same with the resurrection account by Paul.

Another example of this can be found in the Gospel of Mark. In Mark, as Jesus is being led to his crucifixion, a man from the crowd is forced to carry Jesus' cross to the place of execution.

Apparently, the Roman soldiers were in a bit of rush to get the events underway. In Mark 15:21, the author records:

> A certain man from Cyrene, Simon, the father of Alexander and Rufus, was passing by on his way in from the country, and they forced him to carry the cross.

The author, Mark, is rather brief in his Gospel, but here he offers three names and a location—Simon, Alexander, Rufus, and the city of Cyrene. Why does he do this? Richard Bauchkam explains the significance of the record. His words are worth quoting here at length:

> The way Simon is described by Mark—as "Simon the father of Alexander and Rufus"—needs explanation. The case is not parallel to that of Mary the mother of James the little and Joses (Mark 14:40), where the sons serve to distinguish this Mary from others, because Simon (very common though this name was) is already sufficiently distinguished by reference to his native place, Cyrene. Matthew and Luke, by omitting the names of the sons, who that they recognize that. Nor is it really plausible that Mark names the sons merely because they were known to his readers. Mark is far from prodigal with names. The reference to Alexander and Rufus certainly does presuppose that Mark expected many of his readers to know them, in person or by reputation, as almost all commentators have agreed, but this cannot in itself explain why they are named. There does not seem to be any good reason available other than that Mark is appealing to Simon's eyewitness testimony, known in the early Christian movement not from his own firsthand account but through his sons. Perhaps Simon himself did not, like his sons, join the movement, or perhaps he died in the early years, while his sons remained well-known figures, telling their father's story of the crucifixion of Jesus. That they were no longer such when Matthew and Luke wrote would be sufficient explanation of Matthew's and Luke's omission of their names.[2]

---

2. Bauckham, *Jesus and the Eyewitnesses*, 52.

Evidence for the Resurrection

The point here, from both Paul and Mark (and there are others), is that the accounts are written in such a way that the details could easily be verified, and if any deception had taken place, it would be quickly uncovered.

So why would the writers of the Bible offer these details—all of which could be looked into—if they were making it up? Why would they permit readers to have the information that they needed to go and check the writers' sources?

Because it actually happened.

Evidence 3: What Happened to This Paul Guy to Change Him so Much?

When it comes to the Apostle Paul's personal story, we find an argument in favor of the historical reality of the resurrection: Paul's own conversion to Christianity.

Paul is the guy credited with writing over half of the New Testament. He was an influential, gifted, and dynamic leader in the early church who pastored and started churches, trained up leaders, and sent them out to spread this message of Jesus. We can see from his writings that he deeply loved Jesus. In his letter to the church in the city of Philippi, Paul goes so far as to say, "For me to live is Christ, and to die is gain" (Phil 1:21). Paul was nuts about Jesus, claiming that there was nothing in the entire universe that compared with knowing and serving Jesus.

But that wasn't always Paul's story. He talks a lot about his background before coming to faith in Christ, and another New Testament writer, Luke, a doctor, records the type of man Paul was before his conversion.

Paul was a guy who, at one point, went around hunting and killing Christians. As a committed Jew, he felt that Jesus was an imposter, a fraud, and a blasphemer, so Paul eagerly sought to imprison, capture, and sometimes even execute Christians for their allegiance to Jesus. Yet something miraculous happened to Paul that transformed him from a man who hated Jesus to a man who loved him with his whole heart.

The Resurrection and You

Paul recounts exactly what happens to him, recorded by Luke in Acts 22:6–11:

> While I was on my way and approaching Damascus, about noon a great light from heaven suddenly shone about me. I fell to the ground and heard a voice saying to me, "Saul, Saul, why are you persecuting me?" I answered, "Who are you, Lord?" Then he said to me, "I am Jesus of Nazareth whom you are persecuting." Now those who were with me saw the light but did not hear the voice of the one who was speaking to me. I asked, "What am I to do, Lord?" The Lord said to me, "Get up and go to Damascus; there you will be told everything that has been assigned to you to do." Since I could not see because of the brightness of that light, those who were with me took my hand and led me to Damascus.

The difference that Paul experienced, the event that brought about this transformation, according to him, was meeting the resurrected Jesus on the road to Damascus.

Once again, let's be clear. Paul didn't do this for the money, stability, or influence. He had all that in spades before his conversion. After following Jesus, he faced horrible abuse and, really, from a material perspective, didn't gain much at all by becoming a Christian. But something happened in Paul that moved him from being a Jesus hater to somebody who eventually gave his own life for Jesus' sake.

How did this happen? At one point, as Paul is actively looking into this Jesus person, he meets and sees with his own eyes the resurrected Jesus. You can read the account of this in the book of Acts:

> As he (Paul) neared Damascus on his journey, suddenly a light from heaven flashed around him. He fell to the ground and heard a voice say to him, "Saul, Saul, why do you persecute me?" "Who are you, Lord?" Saul asked. "I am Jesus, whom you are persecuting," he replied. "Now get up and go into the city, and you will be told what you must do." (Acts 9:3–6)

Something powerful happened to Paul. Something transformed him entirely. What happened? He became a believer in Jesus because he saw him after he was resurrected!

Evidence 4: "Oh Brother!"

In the book of 1 Corinthians, Paul mentions another individual, named James, who was a witness to the resurrection (1 Cor 15:7). You may or may not be aware of this, but James is Jesus' half-brother. Yes, according to the New Testament, Jesus' mom was a virgin when she gave birth to Jesus. However, Mary was married to Joseph (Jesus' step-dad), and after Jesus was born, as married couples do, they got busy and had other children. So Jesus grew up in a household with half-brothers and sisters, and four times in the Gospels we're told that Jesus' family isn't buying his claims of divinity. In John 7:5 and Mark 3:20–21, we read that Jesus' family didn't believe him and thought he was out of his mind.

Think about this with me: Imagine you're sitting around the dinner table later today and, all of a sudden, your brother-in-law stands up and declares: "I have an announcement to make. I am the son of God." If you're like me, I'm sure you'd be rolling your eyes and saying, "Not again." You wouldn't buy the claim because you know him too well—all his warts, personality quirks, and failed investments. You'd know him too well to buy it. At the very least, if he's a really great guy, you might have to give it some time and see how things play out. Yet James, Jesus' half-brother who witnessed Jesus' life and ministry up close and saw Jesus' crucifixion, somehow goes from being a skeptic to the lead pastor (bishop) of the church in Jerusalem and an influential leader in the early Christian movement. James believed that Jesus was the Messiah, even after growing up in the same house with him! According to church history, James ultimately went to his death proclaiming that his half-brother Jesus really was raised from the dead, and that he was indeed the Son of God.[3]

---

3. Eusebius, *Hist. Eccl.* 2.23.2.

How do you explain this incredible transformation from skeptic to someone who is the lead pastor of a Christian church in Jerusalem and ends up dead for his faith? It wasn't simply seeing his brother crucified—it was witnessing him raised from the dead.

I could present many other arguments about Jesus' resurrection, but I want to keep this book short. Here's what I hope I've accomplished. I want to show you that there's good reason to truly consider Christianity and its central, foundational event—the resurrection. I think in today's world where, for some reason, Christianity has become something that's understood as merely a leap of faith into the unknown, it's important to remember that while faith is involved, it's not a blind or naïve faith. It's important to examine the evidence closely and see that believing in Jesus and the resurrection are, at least, worthy of consideration.

Christianity Invites Critique and Questions

Christianity is a faith that gladly opens itself to examination, questions, and doubts. It's a faith that welcomes the seeker and skeptic because it can hold up to rigorous scrutiny. I offer these few examples to you because I believe it's important that you recognize that wherever you're at in your faith journey, Christianity is not just a blind leap. You can look deeply into this for yourself. You can study it in detail. You can ask the hard questions and the Bible can withstand them.

I push this point because I believe that the resurrection of Jesus is not just true but transformational. It's not simply a concept that we can debate or something that's interesting to ponder, but it has a profound implication for your life right now. If Jesus truly is who he says he is and has risen from the dead, then nothing could be more important Your eternal destiny hinges on your response to this. Examining this for yourself involves asking deeply personal questions and wrestling through and addressing these issues firsthand. Those closest to Jesus believed he rose from the dead. If they believed, what's holding you back?

5

How the Resurrection Answers Our Big Questions

REMEMBER my friend Dave from the introduction? In these types of situations, it's hard to adequately address the innumerable questions that come at you. Instead of arguing forward (say, from the existence of God) to the resurrection, I think we can go about it in the opposite direction.

Apologetics is simply a reasoned defense or justification for a specific belief or theory. In many ways, recent decades have proven to be some of the most rich and fruitful in terms of Christian apologetics. Devout thinkers, philosophers, scholars, and theologians are writing books, posting videos online, and creating content at an incredible rate. While there are many valid forms of apologetics, it can sometimes get a bit tricky trying to understand where to begin.

Why does the resurrection matter? Why is it so central to all that the Bible teaches? Because in the resurrection, the deep, profound, and universal questions we ask as humans are addressed. It's a form of apologetics that works almost in reverse. If the resurrection is possible, then the proverbial cat is "outta" the bag.

The Resurrection and You

In saying this, and in arguing that there is good evidence to believe the historical reality of the resurrection of Jesus, I think it's important to note that coming to the point of believing it, choosing to actually follow Jesus, involves much more than simply accepting intellectual arguments. There is no doubt that *faith* is involved. It must be. Over and over in the Bible, faith is portrayed as the way in which people are called to respond to the Good News of Jesus' resurrection.

> For it is by grace you have been saved, through faith—and this is not from yourselves, it is the gift of God—not by works, so that no one can boast. (Ephesians 2:8)

> For we maintain that a person is justified by faith, apart from works of the law. (Romans 3:28)

So faith is absolutely required and necessary in the Christian life. Now, before you throw up your hands and walk away from the discussion, please understand that this is not an unreasonable expectation. Some people may say, "I prefer fact over faith." While I suppose I understand what they intend, it's not really that simple. Even in your everyday life, you live by faith. Let me give you an example. Are you sitting right now? If so, how do you know that the chair, couch, or seat that you're sitting on could hold you? How did you know that sitting down wasn't a death sentence as the chair collapsed in and around you, leaving you buried under the broken pieces? Well, truth be told, you didn't know. You had a measure of faith in the structural stability and trustworthiness of that chair. The point is that it wasn't a blind faith that you had but a reasonable, justifiable faith. In many ways, it's the same when it comes to Christianity.

Jesus doesn't ask his followers to believe in him with a blind, anti-historical faith. He asks us to consider the evidence, and considering the evidence, place our faith in him. So the question you must ask is not, "Can I know with 100 percent certainty that Jesus rose from the dead?" We can't know very much with 100 percent certainty. To be flippant, you can't even know you're not a computer simulation with 100 percent certainty. You can't know that your spouse of seventy years actually loves you with 100 percent certainty. But in saying all this, I hope the point sticks. You can live your life with honesty and authenticity, believing that the chair will hold you, that you're a real person and not a simulation, and that your faithful spouse, who has never given you reason to doubt, is worthy of trust and truly does love you. One hundred percent certainty—in nearly every area of life—is an unreasonable standard to expect.

So let's work this through.

Does God Exist?

Is there really a God out there somewhere? There are some fantastic resources available that lay out the arguments in favor of God's existence (think cosmological argument, fine tuning argument, human conscience). Those are well and good and absolutely have their place. But let's look at it from a different angle.

If the resurrection of Jesus really and historically took place, then, yes, God exists. Why? Because only God could raise someone from the dead. How else can the reality of physics and natural laws be broken like this? Who else can break them? How else can rot, decay, and rigor mortis be overcome?

Let me put it another way. If the resurrection took place, then it changes the way we perceive what is possible. It didn't occur through a lightning strike à la Frankenstein's monster or through some magic spell from a Harry Potter book. It happened because God is real and was working in human history to raise Jesus from the dead. This is exactly what we read in passages like Acts 2:24, 1 Corinthians 6:14, and Ephesians 1:15-23. The Ephesians reference captures it so well, it's worth quoting in full.

> For this reason, ever since I heard about your faith in the Lord Jesus and your love for all God's people, I have not stopped giving thanks for you, remembering you in my prayers. I keep asking that the God of our Lord Jesus Christ, the glorious Father, may give you the Spirit of wisdom and revelation, so that you may know him

better. I pray that the eyes of your heart may be enlightened in order that you may know the hope to which he has called you, the riches of his glorious inheritance in his holy people, and his incomparably great power for us who believe. *That power is the same as the mighty strength he exerted when he raised Christ from the dead* and seated him at his right hand in the heavenly realms, far above all rule and authority, power and dominion, and every name that is invoked, not only in the present age but also in the one to come. And God placed all things under his feet and appointed him to be head over everything for the church, which is his body, the fullness of him who fills everything in every way.

God the Father raised Jesus from the dead. Only a very real, active, and all-powerful God could do this. The questions of *Does God exist* is answered, at least in part, by the resurrection of Jesus from the dead.

What Happens When We Die?

If Jesus came back from death, he is the one person in all of human history uniquely qualified to talk about the topic of what happens after we die. Over the past decade, there have been no shortage of books written about people dying and getting glimpses or visions of the afterlife. Thank God that horrible genre seems to have exhausted itself and is drying up.

Before his death and resurrection, Jesus talked a lot about heaven and hell. Interestingly, he talked about hell more than anyone else in the Bible. It's always amazing to me how few of these verses make it to plaques or cross-stitches hanging on people's walls.

No one can say that Jesus shied away from talking about the afterlife. He did so on a number of occasions. In the Gospel of Matthew alone, Jesus addresses the topic of hell in 5:22, 29, 30; 10:28; 11:23; 16:18; 18:9; 23:15; and 23:33. For Jesus, the reality of hell is meant to warn us from being complacent or cavalier about our afterlife and to alert us to the reality of a future judgment.

How the Resurrection Answers Our Big Questions

Jesus also talked about heaven. Although he often (in John) used the phrase "eternal life"—which isn't just something to look forward to but something to enjoy now—the point is that the promise for an afterlife with God is brought up time and time again. Passages include John 14:1–6; Matthew 5:12, 6:19–20, 23, 7:21.

Jesus was crucified with two other people. According to the Gospel of Luke, after one of the individuals being crucified called out to Jesus for mercy, Jesus made him a promise: "Truly I tell you, today you will be with me in paradise" (Luke 23:43).

Why does this matter? At some point or another, everyone thinks about death and the afterlife. Do we face eternal nothingness, a void? Do good people go to a good place and bad people to a bad place? How do you even know if you're a *good* person or a *bad* person? How can you be confident about what comes after your heart stops and you move over from the "living" column to the "dead" one? Jesus addressed these questions and claimed to have insight into what comes next and to have done something in his death and resurrection that can give us confidence about what happens to us in the afterlife. The resurrection addresses the big questions that we ask.

The reality is that we're all going to die. The old axiom "No one makes it out alive" is true. Then what? Thankfully, we're not left wondering and guessing about the afterlife. Because Jesus really did die, and really did come back to life, we can trust the one who journeyed on this path before us. The questions of *what happens when I die* is answered, at least in part, by the resurrection of Jesus from the dead.

Does God Really Care? Is God Involved in Human History?

While many people are willing to accept the reality of some form of higher being, the idea that God is both personal and eternal is often a struggle to believe. Is God active in human history? Is he involved in our lives, or is he the grand clock maker who created the world and now stands far off expressing only marginal interest in our affairs?

Atheism denies the existence of God altogether—that there is no higher power, authority, or anything beyond the material. Agnostics may be willing to concede that there is something out there, but that knowing is simply beyond us. Deists, however, believe that while there is likely a God of some sort out there, he more than likely created and removed himself from the picture. The resurrection challenges each of these perspectives.

In the resurrection, we see a God who is not hands-off but hands-on. Jesus was understood to be God-in-the-flesh—the eternal, creating, all-powerful and glorious God come down in human form. All that Jesus said and did reveals to humanity that he was a God who is filled with love, compassion, mercy, and grace. Page after page, the New Testament Gospels (and the whole Bible, for that matter) paint a picture of the investment and concern that God has for the world. He didn't leave us alone, struggling and wondering. He doesn't stand far off, preoccupied with other things. He pursued humanity and was so engaged and invested that he gave his life to rescue us from our brokenness and sin.

The resurrection proves that Jesus really is who he said he is. It demonstrated that God is here! He is active, interested, and working in human history to secure our freedom and offer us life.

Life is hard and often filled with pain and struggle. The natural question we all ask at one time or another is simple: "God, where are you? Do you see? Do you care." In the resurrection, we gain the answers that we seek. God entered into our broken world, lived, died, and rose again so that we could be with him in eternity. God is a God of the impossible. He can bring the dead back to life. He can take your sin, failures, and shortcomings and offer you complete and total forgiveness. He offers hope in our hopelessness. He offers light in the dark. The question *is God involved in human history* is answered, at least in part, by the resurrection of Jesus from the dead.

How the Resurrection Answers Our Big Questions

Is Jesus the Only Way?

The exclusivity of Christ is often one of the most significant hurdles people face when considering Christianity. Why? Because, well, it can just seem so narrow-minded. But this is a point that the Bible is clear on: Jesus is the only way. In Acts 4:12, we read: "Salvation is found in no one else, for there is no other name under heaven given to mankind by which we must be saved." This idea is echoed by Paul in 1 Timothy 2:5. Elsewhere, the author of John puts it this way in what is perhaps the most frequently quoted verse in the Bible: "For God so loved the world that he gave his one and only Son, that whoever believes in him shall not perish but have eternal life." For the writers of the Bible, there's not a lot of wiggle room here. None, in fact.

So why is Jesus unique in his ability to offer salvation? Why can he alone forgive, heal, redeem, deliver, and make us new? Because he alone is God's Son who lived the life that we couldn't and died as our substitute. The resurrection is the evidence that his person (who he was and claimed to be), life (his perfect obedience), and death (as our substitute) have completed the work of salvation. No one else has the resume of Jesus. Of all the religious leaders, teachers, and gurus, only Jesus died and came back from the dead, demonstrating that he was God's anointed, and that God's seal of approval was on him. The resurrection shows us why Jesus alone can offer salvation. The resurrection is God's giant stamp of approval on the payment made for our sins. It's the exclamation point that turns the bad news of Jesus' death into Good News.

Even today, you can visit the graves of various religious founders or "holy men." You can visit the probable sight of Jesus' tomb, but you won't find his bones because death didn't win. In his resurrection, Jesus broke the power of death, and he lives eternally. Because of his resurrection, Jesus alone can offer salvation. The question of *how can Jesus be the only way to salvation* is answered, at least in part, by the resurrection of Jesus from the dead.

The Resurrection and You

Does My Life Matter?

Let me ask you a simple question: Does your life matter? Assuming you're not a committed nihilist, you likely said "yes." Let me follow up with a harder question: If you said "yes," why? Be honest. Why does it matter?

If there is no God, and we come from purposeless chaos and are the product of random atoms smashing together, what hope could we have for understanding our existence and consciousness as anything but abjectly pointless? If matter, time, history, and humanity have no ultimate purpose, how can you? Because we are made in God's image, the vast majority of us live our lives, regardless of what we claim to believe, as if what we do here on earth has some value and meaning beyond us. The majority of people believe that to hurt, kill, rape, and steal is wrong. To care and work for justice, oppose racism, and make the world a better place—these things matter, and we feel it deep in our bones. But once you press a little bit deeper and ask the question of why we feel this way (assuming there is no God), it's hard to justify.

Because of the resurrection of Jesus from the dead, we know that our lives have meaning. It affirms that there is a God and that our lives have value. Why? Because we don't come from nothing nor do we exist without purpose. We are not a cosmic accident or a pointless blip in the universe's timeline. The resurrection affirms for us that humanity has a creator and that this creator came to earth to rescue and free us. Our lives matter because they matter to God. God's love and heart for humanity is displayed in the incarnation (Jesus' coming into human history), his life, death, and life again. God loved us so much that he sent Jesus to do everything necessary to accomplish salvation. Jesus reveals as much when he says, "Greater love has no one than this: to lay down one's life for one's friends" (John 15:13). The questions of *does my life matter* is answered, at least in part, by the resurrection of Jesus from the dead.

Concluding Thoughts

There are very real and significant questions that we naturally ask about life, eternal life, and the claims of Jesus. The problem comes when we avoid asking them honestly, and when we avoid seeking answers. When you step out in the night sky and see the nearly infinite galaxies, when you hold your child for the first time, when you fall in love and walk down the aisle, do you really believe that it all has no purpose? That it's all meaningless? Do you really want to live like nothing you do in this life matters? These questions—What is the purpose of my life? Why am I here? Does my life matter? What happens after I die?—these questions matter. They must be asked and they should be answered.

There are many ways to work through these deep and transcendent questions, but the resurrection of Jesus from the dead as a historical reality offers answers to all of them. These questions are answered in the resurrection. Don't allow your questions about life and your purpose to go unanswered. Don't ignore the deep existential questions about reality; find answers that satisfy and look to the resurrection.

6

The Resurrection of Jesus Is Not Just True, It's Transformational

For the writers of the New Testament, the resurrection of Jesus wasn't just a historical question that was interesting to kick around and debate. The resurrection was the singular event that turned the death of their leader into the "good news." In our Bibles, the term "good news" comes from the Greek word *euangelion*. It was used as a proclamation of victory.[1] Something happened to the early Christians to transform them from fearful, confused followers to bold and daring leaders in the early church. The truth that made the difference in their lives was that Jesus' life, death, and resurrection constituted the "Good News" that God's people had been waiting for. This Good News changed everything!

Good News

Imagine that you were one of the early followers of Christ and had left everything—family, possessions, work—to go and learn from Jesus. Imagine pouring all of your time and energy into learning from Jesus, being with him, and doing what he asked. After a

---

1. C. C. Broyles, in: Green et al., *Dictionary of Jesus and the Gospels*, 282.

The Resurrection of Jesus Is Not Just True

number of years of this, his disciples, understandably, loved him. Now imagine things took a turn for the worse. The guy you've given everything up to follow, the guy you love and respect, is captured and brutally murdered. They were heartbroken. They were distraught. But somehow, this event becomes known as "good news." So what's so good about this story? It's that it's not done. The good news is that he didn't just die—he also rose from the dead.

The resurrection is what turns the most tragic event in human history to the greatest reality you and I can ever imagine. It's the culmination and climax of God's redemptive plan worked out through Jesus.

It's all very strange in one sense. The bloody, gruesome, and violent death of Jesus became the source of confidence and courage for the early Christians. Somehow the events of Good Friday and Easter became the central, defining, and all-consuming truth that Jesus' followers rallied around. They understood their founder's death to be not the worst type of news, but the very best that could ever be imagined. Why is this?

Well, in his resurrection, Jesus demonstrated his victory over three very real, powerful realties that we face today: our sin, death, and the brokenness of the world. His victory over these three enemies is what makes it all Good News. Let's think this through.

Our Sin

The Bible begins with account of creation. God makes all things, speaking them into existence. He makes a man and woman and places them in a garden. Adam and Eve, made in the image of God, are tasked with ruling as God's vice-regents. But disaster strikes. Adam and Eve reject God's kingship and throw their lot in with God's enemy, the devil. This rejection of God's rule is called "sin." To put it simply, "sin" refers to anything that we do, think, or say that robs God of what he's due. It's taking his glory for ourselves, failing to recognize his glory.

Sin is disastrous. The Bible—and our experiences both as a species and individually—display the negative effects of sin.

The Resurrection and You

Relationships break down, violence flourishes, the powerful exploit the weak, and we find ourselves isolated from God and guilty before him. This guilt is nothing to be taken lightly. If God is the creator of all things and the author of life, rejecting him means rejecting life. One biblical author put it this way: "sin leads to death" (Jas 1:5). This death is both physical (we all die) and, perhaps even more tragically, spiritual (we are guilty and separated from God). The spiritual death that the Bible speaks of is often called "hell." Hell is not the place where the bad boys of history will go to party; it's the proper and fitting penalty for those who reject God as king.

You and I—all people—are guilty before God and stand condemned because of our sin. Paul explains this in Romans 3:23: "For all have sinned and fall short of the glory of God." The punishment we face for our rebellion against God is separation from him, eternally, in hell. This is an obviously big deal. So what makes Jesus' death and resurrection Good News?

When Jesus died on the cross, he was acting as our substitute. He willingly stepped into human history, lived a perfect life, and was completely righteous in all things. When he died, he wasn't paying for his own wrongdoings—he was paying for yours. One of Jesus' friends explains it this way:

> For Christ also suffered once for sins, the righteous for the unrighteous, to bring you to God. (1 Pet 3:18)

The good news of the Bible is that Jesus died in our place. He paid the penalty that was due to us. The resurrection is proof that he paid the debt in full. God is our creator and our judge. He's not impartial, given to manipulation, or capricious in his rulings. He is just. So how can a just and holy God overlook our sin? Not by ignoring it or excusing it. The judgment for sin—death—must be met. In Jesus' crucifixion, the judgment that you deserve was paid in full by Jesus. Paul explains this in one of his letters: "having canceled the charge of our legal indebtedness, which stood against us and condemned us; he has taken it away, nailing it to the cross" (Col 2:14). Our sin, shame, and guilt that condemned us was taken away and paid for by Jesus in his crucifixion.

The Resurrection of Jesus Is Not Just True

How can God be both a good and holy judge and, at the same time, be gracious and merciful? If God were to simply ignore sin, take it lightly, or pretend that it didn't matter, he wouldn't be a good or fair judge. Imagine God saying to some of history's most corrupt and evil leaders: "Don't worry. I don't really care that you've murdered, raped, and exploited people. It's not a big deal to me." None of us want a world in which there is no judgment for evil. The problem, if we're honest, is that we want judgment for others—specifically those that we think are worse than us. We want God to judge their sin, and expect that he'll take a different approach when it comes to us. We want a God who judges evil.

But at the same time, if we're honest about our sin and the ways in which we've dishonored God and failed to live for his glory, we're left with a bit of a conundrum. If God is a God who judges sin and evil, what hope is there for us? This is where the Gospel, the Good News, comes into play. How can God be both holy and righteous in his judgment and gracious and merciful? Through Jesus' death on the cross.

Because Jesus died in the cross for you, if you will trust in him, the judgment that was due you is paid in full by Jesus. God didn't ignore sin; he judged it fully and completely in Jesus. There, on that cross, Jesus took our condemnation. We owed a debt, and Jesus paid it all. The Apostle Paul puts it this way: "God made him who had no sin to be sin for us, so that in him we might become the righteousness of God" (2 Cor 5:21). The famous Reformer Martin Luther talked about this in terms of "the great exchange." My guilt for Jesus' righteousness.

Death Itself

Death in all its forms is a destructive, consuming force. One that none of us can escape. We make plans for our life, we set goals and work hard, yet none of us are guaranteed a long life, or even another day. The psalmist in the Old Testament understood this bleak reality. Speaking about death, he says, "When his breath departs, he returns to the earth; on that very day his plans perish" (Ps

146:4). As much as we may try to live our lives with some form of denial about death, we cannot avoid moments when the fragility of life becomes a weighty reality that we have to face. One of Israel's wise sages captured this well, ". . . the living know they will die" (Eccl 9:5). Death is a reality that we all face, one that many of us have felt the sting of. No amount of healthy living, no supplement, no technological or medical invention will remove this haunting reality from the equation.

In 2004, Gianni Pes and Michel Poulain, in the Journal *Experimental Gerontology*, introduced people to what they termed as "blue zones." Five specific locations around the world that had the highest concentrations of centenarians—that is, people who live to be one hundred. While there's much to be learned from their research, and further studies are needed on the diets, habits, and social connectedness of these people, don't miss this one sobering truth—the most you can realistically hope for is one hundred years. On the forefront of the relationship between tech and biology, we're reading about the possibility of everything from consciousness transfers to downloading memories. Even with all these highly advanced technological innovations, we're still fighting against the inevitable finish line that looms in front of us on the horizon—death. Living to one hundred years is quite the accomplishment, but in the grand scheme of eternity, it's nothing. Life is short, often hard, and death awaits us all.

But it wasn't always this way. Originally, God created the world perfect—a place without death. But through sin, death was introduced into creation (Rom 5:12–17). Ever since that day, people are born, live, and eventually die. This is both the curse and punishment of sin. The "wages," or price to be paid for sinning, is death (Rom 6:23).

Jesus the king gave his life for his people, and in his own death and resurrection, he destroyed the power of the grave. What this means is that because death no longer holds power over Jesus (because he's alive!), all who trust in Jesus will likewise share in his life. Those who believe in Jesus and all that he's done are granted

The Resurrection of Jesus Is Not Just True

eternal life and will be raised to new life (like Jesus) on the Last Day. Paul explains this:

> . . . Christ has indeed been raised from the dead, the firstfruits of those who have fallen asleep. For since death came through a man, the resurrection of the dead comes also through a man. For as in Adam all die, so in Christ all will be made alive. (1 Cor 15:20–22)

What this means, practically, for the follower of Christ is that this life is not all we get. Those trusting in Jesus are called to live their lives for God's glory and enjoy whatever gifts he gives them. Yet even though they die, they can die with confidence knowing that this is not the end of the journey but the beginning of a new and great chapter that will never end. John the Apostle puts it like this:

> Whoever believes in the Son has eternal life, but whoever rejects the Son will not see life, for God's wrath remains on them. (John 3:36)

Jesus' resurrection from the dead transforms the way we view not only life but also our death. Death—for those who are trusting in Jesus—is not the end. Because Jesus conquered death, all who are united to him by faith will also conquer death at the resurrection. Paul encourages his friends with these words: "The last enemy to be destroyed [by Christ] is death" (1 Cor 15:26). In his own resurrection, Jesus broke the bonds of death. John Owen cleverly framed it as "the death of death in the death of Christ." This means that for all who trust in Jesus, there will come a day when we can truly sing, "Where, O death, is your victor? Where, O death, is your sting?" (1 Cor 15:55).[2]

---

2. Early church theologian Augustine put it this way: "By the ineffable mercy of God even the penalty of man's offence is turned into an instrument of virtue, and the punishment of the sinner becomes the merit of the righteous. Then death was purchased by sinning; now righteousness is fulfilled by dying . . . God has granted to faith so great a gift of grace that death, which all agree to be contrary of life, has become the means by which men pass into life" (*Civ. Dei.* 13.4).

All of Creation

The opening chapters of the Bible tell the story of God's work in creating the universe. He speaks and it is so. As he was creating, the Bible tells us that God noted that everything he was doing was "good." The world was originally created by God to be a place of perfection. In this perfect world, God's rule and reign as King was to be administered through man and woman, who were placed in the Garden of Eden to tend and manage it (Gen 1:26–30). In the Garden, God placed the Tree of Life and the Tree of the Knowledge of Good and Evil. We aren't told very much about these trees, but God made one thing clear: Adam was not to eat of the Tree of the Knowledge of Good and Evil. This was his one prohibition. God informed Adam that if he ate of that tree, he would die.

You might know what comes next. Adam and Eve are tempted by the serpent, disobey God, and the curse of sin and God's judgment fall over all, including all created matter. Life is corrupted by sin. Everything, every cell and molecule, are subject to this curse. At both an atomic and cosmic level, creation falls under a curse. Like poison running through the body, affecting every part, sin brings ruin, destruction, decay, and death. At the Fall, God pronounces his judgment, and death is introduced into human history. You and I today still experience the effects of Adam and Eve's decision in the Garden. Why do people get sick? Why is cancer such a constant reality? Why do we work hard only to see our plans and efforts flop and fail? Why are there hurricanes and floods that devastate? Genesis provides answers to why we're in the state we're in. It provides answers about why the world we live in is so broken.

All of this over a tree? To you and me it may not seem like that big a deal. But to God, it is. Think about it. God is the King over all. He rules and reigns and his kingdom brings rest, peace, and life. Adam and Eve committed treason in the Garden. They knowingly threw their lot in with God's enemy and set themselves up as rival kings and queens. In essence, their rebellion was stating loud and clear: "You, God, are not my god! I will be my own god!"

The Resurrection of Jesus Is Not Just True

As such, they picked the wrong fight. And they dragged the entire world down with them.

We've already seen that the life, death, and resurrection of Jesus Christ is the grounds by which we are forgiven and rescued from judgment. So does this mean that we can just hunker down, pop open a tube of astronaut food, huddle around a propane cooker in our basements, and wait for the end to come? I mean, if Jesus is coming back some day like the Bible says, aren't we just going to go to heaven and leave this old world behind? Although this is a fairly common understanding of how things are going to play out at the end of time, it's not what the Bible teaches.

Although creation still reveals the glory of God (Ps 19:1–6), it waits to be set right (Rom 8:18–25). The curse of sin will one day be reversed in full at Jesus' reappearing. Part of that incredible day is *recreation*—the New Creation—the ushering in of a new heaven and new earth. This was the hope of Israel's prophets[3] and the early Christians.[4]

What all this means is that God doesn't give up. In the first creation, he entrusted his kingdom administration and rule to his image bearers (Gen 1:27). But we failed. In the New Creation, he entrusts his kingdom to his image bearer (Col 1:15), his Son, Jesus—fully God and fully man. God's not coming up with Plan B. His original intent, to have his people united under his rule, under his image bearer, in a perfect place, will be realized in the New Creation. We are given a glimpse of this in the Bible's closing chapters.

In Revelation 21, after God's final judgment, we're given a picture of God creating the new heavens and earth. You don't need to be a biblical scholar to see the parallels between Revelation 21 and Genesis 1 and 2. The scene painted here is breathtaking. It's a remade world where the stain of sin is completely erased and removed.

Maybe you're thinking, *This is all well and good, but what difference does this make for me?* First, although followers of Christ

---

3. Isaiah 65:17–25.
4. Matthew 5:5; 2 Peter 3:13.

are "citizens of heaven" (Phil 3:20), in the end, we don't end up as disembodied spirits floating around in a spiritual realm. We are decidedly physical and earthy. At the resurrection, believers will be recreated and receive new bodies to enjoy the new creation (1 Cor 15:35–53). This means being able to enjoy the new creation in new (and likely old) ways. It reminds us that our lives here and now have value and purpose. Second, it should go without saying that caring for God's creation should be a priority for Christians. God cares about this world. He is not done and will not give up on it.

When Jesus rose from the dead, it was the defining and inaugural act—step one in God's plan to fix what was lost in the Fall. The good news that we gather from this is that God doesn't give up—not on creation, not on his plan, and not on you.

Putting It All Together:

Jesus' resurrection from the dead addresses our greatest needs. We are sinners, guilty before God. Jesus is the means by which we can be forgiven and accepted by God. We live our lives with the reality that one day we will draw our last breath. Death is something we can't escape. Jesus' resurrection from the dead, his victory over death, is our source of confidence that our own death is not the end and that all who trust in Jesus will not be defeated by the grave. We live in a broken world. Sure, it can be beautiful, fun, and thrilling, but it's just not what it should be. Jesus' resurrection is the "firstfruits" of the harvest of God's work to recreate all things.

That's why Jesus' death and life again are called "Good News." Jesus' life, death, and resurrection are the means by which our sin is atoned for, our eternity secure, and our future filled with hope. This is the Good News that the Bible teaches. The question you have to answer is this: What are you going to do with the Good News?

7

The Resurrection and You

THIS Good News about Jesus' life, death, and resurrection calls for a response. It's not something you can remain neutral to. Jesus invites us to respond to his kingship in two ways: faith and repentance (Mark 1:15). It may be helpful to think about these two responses as really being one, like two sides of the same coin.

Faith means believing and trusting in what God has said to be true. Faith is trust, and it's only as good as the object of its trust. It means taking God at his word and believing the Good News about Jesus. Repentance means turning away from what is false. For some, this means turning away from false gods and worshiping the one true God. For some, it means turning away from looking to "self" as king and recognizing that God alone is King. Or maybe it means turning away from looking to sin or destructive habits to provide your life with meaning, purpose, and joy. Simply put, responding to the Good News with faith and repentance means turning towards Jesus in trust and belief.

If you're still with me and you're not a follower of Christ, if you haven't responded with faith and repentance, make today the day that you do. Pay close attention to the words of Paul: "Today is the day of salvation" (2 Cor 6:2, quoting Isa 49:8).

The Resurrection and You

We must place our trust in Jesus alone, calling out to him for salvation. We must come to the end of ourselves and say to him: "I'm done. I could never earn favor with you. I have no righteousness of my own to claim. I have no right to be a child of God, yet I see what you have done on the cross and through your resurrection, and I trust in that alone." When God opens our eyes and we obey by responding with faith and repentance, something incredible happens. Jesus' spotless record of obedience, faithfulness, and goodness is given to us. And our sin, shame, and failures—all the perversions, lies, and evil that you and I have ever done—are taken by Christ and paid for. That's the Good News. That's the miraculous hope that the resurrection offers to us.

If you're reading this and you would say "I'm an old faithful, Deven. I've been a Christian for years now," then let me encourage you. Your faith does not rest on myth or wishful thinking. You can test it and examine it deeply. Your faith can be strong, and it can withstand the skeptics and your own doubts. Take confidence in that. If you're reading this and consider yourself a Christian but Jesus isn't central to your life, I want to challenge you. If you believe this message, do you really think that Jesus died a horrible death and rose victorious over sin, over death, over hell, and over the grave so that he could be a footnote in your life? If you're truly a Christian, you belong to him. He purchased you with his blood, and you will never find joy trying to live in two worlds. Find a solid Christian community that loves Jesus, follows his Word, and is active in mission, and then throw some roots down so that you can grow.

And finally, if you're reading this and you are not a follower of Jesus, I want to push you to have the courage to look into this for yourself. But let me warn you—there are supernatural and spiritual forces that don't want you to do this. They don't want you to examine this deeply. They will seek to find ways to distract you from this pursuit or provide excuses to prevent you from looking into this. Have the courage to press on in your investigation of this. What the Bible says is true, and it's the most important thing you

The Resurrection and You

could ever address and the most crucial question that could ever be answered.

The best way that I know of to work through the claims and implications of the Good News of Jesus' death and resurrection is first to read the Bible for yourself. Second, I highly encourage you to find a church community you can connect with and begin the process of learning and growing. When you're seeking out a church community, find one that actually believes what the Bible teaches. There's really no point in going to a so-called "church" that spends the majority of its time explaining how the Bible doesn't mean what it says. Tragically, these types of churches are far too common. So grab a Bible and find a church. What's incredible is that God's Spirit moves and works through his Word and through his people. As you read and study, and as you develop relationships and engage with a church community, God will meet you in that journey.

If this is all true, if Jesus really did rise from the dead, then there is nothing else that could be more important. Sure, it's important to wrestle through your vocation, your education, to think deeply about life's big decisions: who will you marry, how you invest your money, and so forth. But nothing matters more than the person, claims, and the death and resurrection of Jesus. Paul, in 1 Corinthians 15:3-4, explains this:

> For what I received I passed on to you as of first importance: that Christ died for our sins according to the Scriptures, that he was buried, that he was raised on the third day according to the Scripture

Here, he calls the truth of the resurrection as being of "first importance." I really couldn't agree more.

So let me end with this: What will you do with the resurrection?

Bibliography

Bauckham, Richard. *Jesus and the Eyewitnesses: The Gospels as Eyewitness Testimony.* Grand Rapids, MI: Eerdmans, 2008.
Bruce, F. F. *New Testament History.* New York: Galilee/Doubleday, 1980.
Crossan, John Dominic. *The Power of Parable: How Fiction by Jesus Became Fiction about Jesus.* New York: Harper One, 2013.
Crossley, James G. *The Date of Mark's Gospel: Insight from the Law in Earliest Christianity.* New York: Bloomsbury T. & T. Clark, 2004.
D'Costa, Gavin, ed. *The Baseless Fabric of a Vision, Michael Goulder.* London: Oneworld, 1996.
D'Costa, Gavin. *Resurrection Reconsidered.* Oxford: Oneworld, 1996.
Dix, T. Keith, and George W. Houston. "Public Libraries in the City of Rome: From the Augustan Age to the Time of Diocletian." *Mélanges de l'école Française de Rome* 118.2 (2006) 671–717. https://doi.org/10.3406/mefr.2006.10261.
Ehrman, Bart. *Did Jesus Exist? The Historical Argument for Jesus of Nazareth.* New York: HarperOne, 2012.
Evans, Craig A. *Jesus and His World: The Archaeological Evidence.* Louisville, KY: Westminster John Knox, 2013.
Goodyear, Sheena, "He thought he was crashing at his Airbnb. It turned out to be a stranger's guest house." https://www.cbc.ca/radio/asithappens/as-it-happens-the-thursday-edition-1.6388702/he-thought-he-was-crashing-at-his-airbnb-it-turned-out-to-be-a-stranger-s-guest-house-1.6388767
Green, Joel B., et al. *Dictionary of Jesus and the Gospels.* Downers Grove, IL: InterVarsity Academic, 1992.
Habermas, Gary R. *The Historical Jesus: Ancient Evidence for the Life of Christ.* Joplin, MO: College Press, 1996.
Hyer, Marjorie. "Colson Preaches That Watergate Proves the Bible." *Washington Post*, September 28, 1983. https://www.washingtonpost.com/archive/local/1983/09/28/colson-preaches-that-watergate-proves-the-bible/e4978ba1-795b-44ed-b9e8-2cfe90e6e2d2/.

Bibliography

Johnson, William A., and Holt N. Parker. *Ancient Literacies: The Culture of Reading in Greece and Rome.* New York: Oxford University Press, 2009.

Keener, Craig. *The Historical Jesus of the Gospels.* Grand Rapids, MI: Eerdmans, 2009.

Ladd, George Eldon. *A Theology of the New Testament.* Grand Rapids, MI: Eerdmans, 1974.

Licona, Michael R. *The Resurrection of Jesus: A New Historiographical Approach.* Downers Grove, IL: InterVarsity, 2010.

Moriarty, Michael. *Pascal: Reasoning and Belief.* Oxford: Oxford University Press, 2020.

Polhill, Dr John B. *Paul and His Letters.* 1st ed. Nashville, TN: Broadman and Holman, 1999.

Scripture Index

OLD TESTAMENT

Genesis

1	55
2	55
1:27	55

Psalms

19:1–6	55

146:4	52

Ecclesiastes

9:5	52

Isaiah

49:8	57

NEW TESTAMENT

Mathew

5:12	43
5:22	42
5:29	42
5:30	42
6:19–20	43
6:23	43
7:21	43
10:28	42
16:18	42
23:15	42
23:33	42
27:57	32
27:57–61	27
27:60	21
28:1–10	17, 31
28:10	22
28:12–14	24
28:16	22

Mark

1:15	57
3:20–21	37
14:40	34
15:21	34

Luke

22:54–62	17
23:50–51	27
23:43	43
24:1–12	17
24:2	21
24:11	17
24:12	18

63

Scripture Index

John

3:36	53
7:5	37
14:1–6	43
15:13	46
20	25
20:24–25	25
20:26–28	25

Acts

2:24	41
4:12	45
9:3–6	36
22:6–11	36

Romans

3:23	50
3:28	40
5:12–17	52
6:23	52
8:18–25	55

1 Corinthians

6:14	41
15	2, 15
15:1–8	32
15:3–4	59
15:7	37
15:6	15
15:20–22	53
15:26	53
15:25–55	56
15:55	53

2 Corinthians

| 5:21 | 51 |

| 6:2 | 57 |

Ephesians

| 1:15–23 | 41 |
| 2:8 | 40 |

Philippians

| 1:21 | 35 |
| 3:20 | 56 |

Colossians

1:15	55
2:6–8	6
2:14	50

1 Timothy

| 2:5 | 45 |

2 Timothy

| 3:12 | 5 |

James

| 1:5 | 50 |

1 Peter

| 3:18 | 50 |

2 Peter

| 1:3 | 6, 17 |

Revelation

| 21 | 55 |

64

Made in the USA
Coppell, TX
28 October 2022